Poetic Memoirs

Poems from a Caribbean Perspective

PEARL E. HANLEY

Book Vine Press
2516 Highland Dr.
Palatine, IL 60067

Contents

Children

Education

Celebration

Black History

Christmas

Creative Writings

Miscellaneous

Be An Overcomer!

Tributes

Poetic Memoirs Part 2

Hurricanes

COVID - 19

What A Life: What A World: What A Time!

Our Presidents

Prologue

Preface

These poems express experiences that I have encountered in life:
Both in Nevis where I was born, grew up,
schooled, worked and gave birth.
And in St. Thomas, United States Virgin Islands where I now reside.
If you can identify with any of them I trust you
will find it beneficial and be blessed.
I know Nevisians can recall many of them.

Love you all. Enjoy!

Inspiration

Trust in the Lord with all your heart and lean not to your own understanding. In all your ways acknowledge Him and He will direct your paths. Proverbs 3:5-6

I'll Be

I'll be what You want me to be, Dear Lord,
I'll do what You want me to do.
Show me my role in this suffering world,
I know I can depend on You.

I'll go where You want me to go, Dear Lord,
I'll say what You want me to say.
Teach me to obey Your Great Command
So, the best can be made of my stay.

Mercy, Not Justice St. John 8:4-11

Jesus, I too read how they brought the accused,
Expecting You to condemn, not refuse or excuse.
They were ready to cast stones to her head,
Stones of sin and kill her dead.

But You in love wrote on the ground,
Waiting for someone without sin to be found
So, convicted they departed – consumed with guilt,
Without being cleansed, and still in their filth
Though filled with shame, they would not accept blame.

Then the accused in the spirit of repentance
Your forgiveness offered, she claimed acceptance.
"Go and sin no more," You humbly plead,
"I do not condemn you, please turn from a life of greed.
And come unto Me, all you who are in need."

**There is therefore now no condemnation to them who are in
Christ Jesus, who walk not after the flesh, but after the Spirit.**
Romans 8:1

The cross makes the difference for me.

SONG: **There's room** at the cross for you. (2X)
        Though millions have come
        There's still room for one.
        Yes, there's room at the cross for you.

The following poem, "Thank You Lord" and song, "God Bless America" were penned after Hurricane Marilyn's fury in 1995.

Thank You Lord!

I was sick and in deep despair,
I cried unto You, Lord, and You heard my prayer.
When I thought I would be blind,
You were so mercifully kind.

Thanks to Dr. Thomas who took care of me.
He came all the way from Hawaii.
And he was as kind as You would be.
You gave him wisdom, You gave him power,
To help me in that crucial hour.

It's been several days now, and the trauma has parted.
With the first application, I knew a miracle had started.
I could open my eye I could face the light.
The pain now gone; the outlook seems bright.
THANK YOU, LORD!

But the other eye said, "Not so fast,"
My fame and glory is here at last.
So, it became red, it became painful,
To see them both was very shameful.

The competition was enormous!
Each trying to see which could be worse.
The redness, the pain, water springing again,
From eye to eye like the changing weather,
And both eyelids glued together.

I could not clean the Church,
I could not drive or go to service.
I just stayed home and thanked God for His goodness
Now back to the doctor I go for more tests,
I know everything will work out for the best.
Thank You Lord!

In conclusion, I would just like to say,
Take care of your health in every way.
High cholesterol, diabetes, or high blood pressure
Can make an illness seem to last forever!

God Bless America

God bless America, land that I love
May You guard her and guide her,
With Your blessings from above.
From the mountain to the valley
From the ocean to the sky
God bless America, my home sweet home,
God bless America, my new adopted home.

God bless America, land of the free
Protect her and direct her,
As she praises You on bended knee.
From Fema to Vitema,
From the Red Cross to the Boss.
God bless America, land of the free,
God bless America, our aid to recovery.

God bless America, home of the brave,
Forgive her and live in her,
As You pardon and heal and save.
From the president to the Congress
From Legislator to Governor,
God bless America, home of the brave,
God bless America, pardon, heal and save.

My Gratitude:

Please excuse my platitude
I just wished to broaden my latitude,
To express a note of gratitude.
I did not mean to procrastinate,
Time and thought were needed to cultivate,
The kind of language that would generate,
A worthy response for all the gifts
That truly my humble spirit lifts.

To: The St. Thomas/St. John Federation of Teachers
AFT: Local 1825
On my Retirement: August 31, 2004

Events

The Tremors: December 26, 1950 – January 2, 1951

Light earthquakes were a regular thing.
And coming that day was really no big thing,
But the quakes became more violent and heavy,
As the evening approached, nothing was steady.
The earth rumbled, opened, and shook
And things fell from every cranny and nook.

Stone buildings tumbled to the ground,
Leaving pain and devastation all around
A vacuum came to life in Cades Bay,
With water boiling rapidly, night and day.

The tremors were felt in neighboring isles.
Officials came to query from across the miles.
The culprits were reprimanded, and made to redeem,
Could you believe Mr. Barber wanted to block the bath stream?

Tents were erected in the school yard,
So education would continue without being marred.
It lasted for a while which was good and great,
But the situation wasn't ideal or first rate.

Restoration was fast and quick,
And soon we were back in our brand-new brick.
Reading, writing, arithmetic and more
Learning important lessons that youths should store.

12-26-1950 – 01-02-1951

Mv. Christina

THE morning of August 1, 1970
Is a memorable one for my sister, my two
sons and me.
We were so excited to be going away,
All four of us boarded the boat that day.
The sea was rough, and the waves were high.
The boat rocked as we waved goodbye.

Our cousin took us to the airport,
"Sorry to leave but I have to catch the boat.'
Then remarked, "If I could do it again.
I would have definitely caught the plane."

So off he went to his final destiny,
As we watched the boat sailing unknowingly.
The overloaded vessel was surely a crime,
But clearly the captain didn't give a dime.

Intended passengers fussed and fumed,
The officers said there was no more room.
The vessel is too full, don't you see!
But they had to get home for the holiday ceremony.

Halfway in the journey, in the middle of the ocean
The waves became boisterous, the boat leaned to the motion.
Water splashed inside to the heaving tide,
And passengers began moving all to one side.

The elite were in the captain's quarter.
Drinking, and gambling, having fun and laughter.
The boat was going under, and they were trapped.
Without a clue of how to get free or unwrapped.

Facing sure death, and no rescue for the perishing.
Despite the screaming, shoving, and shouting!
But to no avail - they just lay there dying.
HOW SAD!

No life jackets on board and many could not swim
There was no time to pray or even sing a hymn.
As people went under, sharks emerged in teams,
And ripped off limbs, despite all the screams.

A few were able to swim ashore.
Then help came and rescued some more.
Children lost their parents; families were no more.
What an awful holiday was then in store.

Despite all the chaos, turmoil, and destruction
Many gave thanks although with much emotion.
The Christina now at the bottom of the ocean,
Many take trips to see this great phenomenon.

THANKS BE TO GOD!!
August 1, 1970

Marilyn

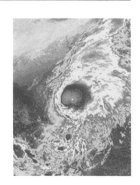

September 1995 was a memorable night,
When Marilyn appeared and darkened our sight
But after lashing St. Croix at first
She flew over and pounded us with her curse.

We were not expecting a Category Four.
"Would be Category Two," they said, "and no more."
But after feeling Marilyn's fury
We didn't need a decision by a jury.

The screaming, the crying as off the roofs blew,
My apartment is flooding, they called the radio too.
The only safe place is the bathroom you see,
All huddled together my children and me.

Outside the rains pour, while the winds roar
Lifting the louvers and watering the floor.
The building shook I imagined in fear.
But by morning others confirmed the idea.

Devastation was here, there, and everywhere.
Trees were like sticks their branches were bare.
The howling winds sent debris crashing and eroding,
We were afraid of windows and doors exploding.

Solar panels were ripped from the roofs.
Cars and trucks showed visible proofs.
Garbage receptacles blocked the road,
And vehicles piled high resembling the shipping mode.

Our favorite supermarket was no more.
Grand Union was really a special store.
Made of steel - who would have thought,
It could have twisted and crumbled and come to naught.

Many places we did not know were there,
Became clearly visible as if out from nowhere.
Expensive property up on the hills
Were blown away, imagine the bills!

Help came from the United States,
Food, medicine, even radio to communicate.
We give God thanks for all He has done,
And the many blessings, especially His Son.

"Thank God for life again" was the popular refrain!

The Fire 10-21-73

It was a warm night in October,
As far as I can remember.
Five families were asleep peacefully,
When my mother awoke and went to see.

She followed the crackling sound to the porch.
What she saw was frighteningly the worse
Having a fire raging right under our nose
She proceeded to wake sleepers from their repose.

We got out with just the clothes on our backs,
Even a baby had escaped the attacks.
Then we watched from a nearby resident
As flames consumed the wooden tenement.

All was lost except the washing machine,
Which was housed outside in a concrete bin.
The Maynard's were able to save a couch
But nothing else could enter their pouch

We were driven to Frenchtown Community Center
Where we stayed until the next day to enter,
The Bovoni Housing. Buildings E and D
Which became our home but not for free.

I would always cherish the time spent there,
For when I became homeless and had nowhere
They opened the doors and invited us to stay,
For years to come day after day.

GOD BE PRAISED!

FIRE AND WATER: GOOD SERVANTS – BAD MASTERS!

October 21, 1973

Children

Children: A Gift From God

Children are a special gift,
Sent to us from God above.
So, we must nurture and cherish them
With compassion, care, and love.

Children are our most precious resource,
We often hear them - the politicians say...
But fall short of financially leading the way,
With laws that end in pain and remorse.

We must not let our children drift,
Into this world's sin and Satan's lies,
For he will crush and trample and sift
Their innocent mind until it dies.

Let God ever be our guide and stay,
For He has taught us how to pray,
And train our children the right way.
That we may be true to Him day by day.

Children, obey your parents in the Lord,
That is what the Scriptures say.
So, you can have a long, and fruitful life,
And live the Christian way - day after day.

Kindergarten And More

Jane E. Tuitt Elementary School
A place that enforced the Golden Rule
It taught the children to be good and kind,
Caring and sharing with a loving mind.

The kindergarten teacher taught her children well,
With various disciplines, involving show and tell.
Physical Education and play, keep the body active,
But reading and writing were solid and massive.

Field trips to Coral World and more were social events,
Children learned speech and proper English comments.
Birthday parties and songs were fun and exciting,
Making classes and rest time so very inviting.

Other grades were extremely challenging,
Substituting for teachers was harassing and demanding,
For children tried and tested your faith
To see how and if you will retaliate.

Many times, I wanted to quit.
Having discipline was not in their spirit.
But I held on despite the torture
That's when I decided not to be a teacher.

However, I went to college and took classes at CVI,
In subjects I thought would be beneficial,
But four years of study with memory loss, to heed
I thought it better spent teaching children to read.

Here I am now retired and all,
Living my life and having a ball.
Helping, sharing, caring, and loving
All the students who made my career interesting.

Green – My Color

Green is a color, a color just for me.
Even though people can't see, it reminds me of a tree.
I like how green looks after it rains on the grass,
I like green, I think it's a blast.
I would wear green to Prom-night or to class.
I really would – why would you ask?
I would even wear green as a bridesmaid dress,
I really think it relieves the stress!
I would have green for the therapeutic ball,
It's everything green when I hit the mall.
I have and play a green clarinet,
I would like to catch a green butterfly in a net.

I would have green on my bed, on my head,
And even when I'm dead.
Green could go with every color in the book,
If you haven't noticed, take a look.
I don't understand why people don't like green,
I would wear that on my team.
Green is a color – a color just for me,
If you like green you should join us, THE GREEN TEAM!

BY: HADIYA HANLEY (7 years)

Education

My Philosophy

My philosophy on education is simply this:
To educate the whole child – mind, body, soul and spirit.
With academics, music, and spiritual guidance
Coupled with punctuality and daily attendance.

Discipline is the key for learning to take place.
So, students be wise in running the race.
Listen to your teachers, exercise self-control, show interest,
In what is being taught - and having respect.

Respect for self, for classmates and for teachers
Knowing in the end you will be the reapers.
Teachers too, must be disciplined to do their part,
So, everything will go well right from the start.

Punctuality, regular attendance, and lesson plans preparation
Are outstanding work ethics for a timely demonstration!
Teaching should always be a pleasant experience,
Where children learn, play, and grow with intelligence.

Education too must cater to all,
Not all students though are college called,
Innovative programs in divers disciplines
Make for a society of honest and productive citizens.

School Time
In Queen City

NEVIS, the isle of serenity and beauty
Is also known as the magical Queen City.
Beauty pageants and shows, their creativity unfolds,
With the lovely and talented local schoolgirls.

Many disciplines were taught in our schools,
So, we would not grow up to be absolute fools.
Academics, foreign language, and impromptu speech
Success, faithfulness, and independence teach.

The principals were very demanding.
Teaching by rote without understanding.
So, forgetting a word would throw us off base,
And defeat the whole purpose of the Black human race.
Which made them outrageous instead of courageous,
All puffed up with pride without God as their guide.

Some teachers were challenging, others a challenge.
Sheer diligence and determination got some to college.
Lack of classroom control even with academic knowledge
To the teacher infuriating - for the student frustrating.

A walking encyclopedia is what we called **Brother B**
For he knew every word and meaning in the English dictionary.

One teacher in particular right from the start
Had no idea what he should impart.
The entire period he talked sports with the boys,
While ignoring us girls as mere discarded toys.
And when the bell signaled time to leave again
"So far so good" was his parting refrain.

Geometry was taught by the preacher's wife.
Fifth Form was the end of our High School life.
She taught the blackboard with her back to the class,
Not caring that we have exams to pass.
Talking, and writing, then immediately erasing.
No time to discuss, answer questions, or review.
So, our books we took home on our own to pursue.

My favorite teacher, Mrs. Stevens, was so good,
She taught her classes as a real teacher should.
The Scriptures came to light, made Mathematics a delight.
For when our faces revealed we did not understand
She explained again and again without reprimand.
English too was a blast, and all her classes we did pass.

A Gem of Knowledge deserves an Emblem of Courage.

The Excitement:

I remember quite vividly that day in class,
When a helicopter wanted to land on the grass.
But landed instead in the nearby park.
Thus, creating a ruckus while making its mark.

People came from all over to see,
What this great flying machine could be.
So down to the park we children did run,
Despite the Principal calling "The day is not done!"

Local war veterans their knowledge display
While listening to what the officers had to say.
We learned many important lessons that day.
But then it rose and flew away.

Grove Park is also famous for cricket -
Where tournaments are all about runs and wicket.
So, come and enjoy the 'fours' and the 'sixes'
For in this our culture one relaxes.

The time of our classes would not be the same,
So, we children could go and enjoy the game.
From seven in the morning to one in the afternoon,
Was the same length of time spent in the classroom!

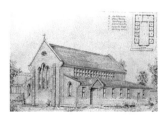

Back To School:
By Harmonie Hanley

Back to school is the theme,
Of the poem I must redeem.
Back to school means coming from vacation,
So, I should tell you about the occasion,
For Miami, Florida was our destination.

The experience was fantastic,
Recalling it seems almost unrealistic.
Theme parks, the rides, the food, the fun
And all so pleasant in the Florida sun.

Now back to school is my destination,
So, I must face it with anticipation.
Academics, Art, Music, and Physical Education,
Make it possible to look forward to graduation.
I must be diligent, work hard, and never give up.
To home and school teachings, I must live up.

August 2012

Ariel And Alexis

Two little girls both three and five
Came to stay with Grandma for a while.
They were so cute and cuddly and alive,
So, she took them everywhere in style.

They enjoyed playing in the summer sun,
While romping with classmates and having fun.
But when wintertime came around
They expected to see snow on the ground.

"Where is the snow"? They would ask,
"We have to perform our winter task –
Making snow angels and building snowmen,
Instead of playing games with Auntie Gwen."

In day school we learned very well
We brought in objects for show and tell.
We learned to read, and we learned to write,
Some would even say we were very bright.

When Grandma took us shopping in the store
We read all the greeting cards and lots more.
But going to the bank was even more fun,
To see bills and money shooting up the chute
Like bullets from an automatic gun.

Grandma bought us pretty dresses,
To go to Church and hear Bible stories.
And the message how Jesus died on the cross,
To save us from sin so we won't be lost.
The music, the singing, and the mime dancing
Were important lessons they were teaching.

In Sunday - School we learned Bible verses
Memorized them and the reference too,
Recited poems, celebrated Christmas in the Churches
And worshipped the Creator and gave Him His due.

Jesus is the reason for the Season!

The Crossroads:

Youths at the crossroads could find a scary place.
Not knowing which way they should take.
For there is danger lurking in every space
If the wrong turn they may ever make.

Many wolves in sheep's clothing are lurking there,
Scheming and perfecting their plans everywhere.
Of how to pounce on young innocent youths
With their very smooth talk and flashy suits.

They observe where there is vulnerability,
Making the answer to the problem a possibility.
So, they can manipulate the unsuspecting mind,
Into thinking that they are just being kind.

The crossroads is a confusing place,
Especially if you want to run the race.
So many roads from which to choose,
If not careful you can really lose.

So be vigilant, be sober, and of a sound mind,
For honesty and decency are hard to find,
In a sinful world so full of crime and lust
Seeking Christ is an absolute must.

JESUS is the answer for the world today,
Without Him there's no other, Jesus is the way.

Celebration

Celebrate!

April 19, is here at last,

I can't believe it has come so fast.

Four Score years is what it brings

To that special lady who so sweetly sings.

Give me my flowers she'd always say

While I am living to see that day.

God has been good, and she is here

Her children made sure

With her friends she can share.

HAPPY 80TH **SISTER VAL!**

    1933 - 2013

    STILL GOING STRONG 1N 2021!

    To God be true in 2022.

A Centurian: Ms. Ann

GOD BLESS you as we remember your birth,

ONE HUNDRED years here on this earth.

FEBRUARY EIGHTEEN was the date

And you came not a minute late.

1914 - 2014 makes you a **GRAND FIVE SCORE –**

That is **ONE CENTURY** and hopefully more.

So, celebrate and have a blast,

Your special day is here at last.

Why? Yo**u your Savior will not pass**

For you are a woman of class.

HAPPY BIRTHDAY – AUNT M.

   STILL GOING STRONG IN 2021!

    To God be true in 2022.

A Gift

Hadiya Janay is her name.
She is a young girl of fame.
She plays in her school's marching band,
And also tunes on the steel pan.
The clarinet though is her passion,
She could make music her profession.

She has been a whiz academically,
From pre-school to presently.
Has always been Number One in class
For all her exams she does pass.

Then while relaxing in the lobby,
She writes poetry as a hobby.
A contestant in the Spelling Bee
And Valedictorian in Elementary.

Whatever her decision,
She will have a mission,
For she heeded the call
And tried out for Basketball.
A member of Muller's Garden Club
After which she needed a good scrub.
And a participant in Sunrise Kids Triathlon.

So before going any further,
This gifted and talented person
Is really my granddaughter.

The Walk Of Fame
July 2012

WAY, WAY back in 1942,
When the sky was azure blue
A little girl whose name is Purl,
Was born in the morn,
At the beginning of the dawn.

She became a girl of action,
Even though just a fraction.
Dancing and prancing on the pier,
With her long black flowing hair.
Her mother, the seamstress, made all her clothes,
From her head, right down to her toes.

Mr. Kirton, our French teacher in High School
Thought that he was so cool,
Making fun of her knock knees
And mimicking the way she ran in the breeze.
By rubbing together with his wrists,
Trying to make some mysterious tricks.

Seventy years later in 2012
The knees are all straight and quite themselves.
Thanks to Dr. Davis, Dr. Bacot and their crew,
And nurses at Schneider and Sea View too.
For she is now as good as new.

Horizon too, needs much mention
For they really helped to ease the tension.
Mary, Eileen, Chris and Lindsay
Along with their accountant and secretary.

Therapists in all three locations
Did their part to achieve this transformation.
So, Mr. Kirton if you could see her now
You couldn't help but take a bow.

Hurrah For Seaview:

TEN YEARS AGO, in the
year two thousand two
I was whisked away from hospital to Seaview
The ambulance took me to a new scenery
For total knee replacement therapy.

Three weeks of Denise's measuring team
That menacing ruler did make me scream.
To feel the extra push and see it unfolding
I wished it lost, broken, or stolen.

The treatment was long and painful
But the staff was extremely careful.
Nurse Monsanto from St. Thomas and the one from St. John
That experience was just a natural phenomenon.
The **way** they bathed the intricate part
When I couldn't help myself or muster the heart.
Not all though were that accommodating,
But still I gave the institution a very good rating.

Today everyone is doing his part
To see everything runs smoothly right from the start.
The therapists both times took their work seriously
For even Chris remembers me.
Denise and Cara, their career though their passion,
Yet on the job show tremendous compassion.

Walking the stairs is a science but a breeze -
Knowing which foot to step on first, without hurting the knees.
The wheelchair, then the walker, are tools to ease the pain,
But on your discharge, you need only a cane.
I particularly liked the knee bending machine,
So relaxing, so comforting, though exercise is foreseen.

Black History

A Caribbean Anthem

ISLANDS in the West Indies,
Line the Caribbean Seas.
Land of beauty with white sand beaches,
And green, green trees.

The nature of the people
Is gentle and serene,
They greet you with good morning,
And a smile that lights the scene.

Though we are different peoples
Of nation, color, and creed
United we stand together,
For in our culture, we are freed.

The uniqueness of our culture,
Speaks of who we are.
Our heritage we proudly embrace:
These islands are in God's grace.

Written by: Patricia Cannonier Robb

God bless our Caribbean and its peoples,
Who labored hard and build famous steeples.
From our native land we were taken
But trusting God we are never forsaken.

WE ARE ONE CARIBBEAN: ONE PEOPLE!

A Tribute To: Dr. Martin Luther King Jr.

Patterned after Psalm 103

1. I will thank the Lord for Dr. Martin Luther King Jr.
2. and will always remember his accomplishments.
3. He has helped Blacks and Whites to unite and to bring an end to racism. That WAS his aim. He was dedicated to the cause.
4. He preached equality through his ministry.
5. God is great. God is forgiving.
6. He gave Dr. King the grace to forgive his enemies.
7. He loved everyone no matter their skin color. He was color blind.
8. His love for people was as deep as the ocean and as wide as the seas.
9. Thank You Lord for Dr. Martin Luther King Jr.

Composed 1/15/06 by:
The Junior Sunday-School Class of Bovoni Baptist Church

Principles Of Black History:

Black History is a commemoration of bravery,
And freedom from the bondage of slavery.
A celebration of what is right and fair,
Is a life we all can and should share!

Brave men like Gandhi, Mandela, and King
Fought with words as they march and sing.
Though rocks and blocks the bones may break
They never could our freedom take.

Great men of color have contributed,
Many disciplines were then instituted.
Agriculture, medicine, household goods and more
That we can buy in the neighborhood store.

Unity, strength, and honor have we,
For all the world our courage to see.
Creativity, faith, purpose, all working together,
With self-determination, while helping each other.

God be thanked for each activist,
Who helped our culture to exist?
So, we can live a better life,
Without undue worry, war, or strife.

These are vital principles and attributes,
And we should strive to acquire these attitudes.
For God would have us respect each other
Mother, sister, father, or brother.

The Human Race:

GOD made us in His own image,
This we can count as a great privilege.
We are all of the same Human Race,
That God on this earth has put in place.

Red and yellow, black and white
We are all very precious in God's sight.
For He made Adam and Eve with genes
That can produce various colors and means.

There is no race called White or Black,
'Twas only a ploy to dominate and whack,
Color, culture, creed and courage
Are people groups we should acknowledge!

Black was really the original color,
With varying shades that make the skin lighter
Depending on the region they chose to relocate,
After Babel - in frigid, torrid, or temperate climate.

Just as animals have functions that differ,
Some fly, crawl, swim, walk, hop and slither.
And plants display their beauty with a variety-
Of shapes, uses, and colorful shades in the society.

SONG: Every nation, every tribe and tongue
Coming together in Jesus as one,
We may come from different places,
Some are cold, some have tropical skies.
We may have many different faces.
Some are brown, some have slanted eyes.
In God there is no difference
For we are created in His image.

The History Of The Islands

NOW listen as the story is told,
How the **Virgin Islands** were bought and sold.
Way back when **Columbus** came,
The New World was what he claimed.
The **Caribs and Arawaks** were Indians here,
Who roamed the land with freedom - then fear!

November 14, 1493, is an important date in history,
For when the **Spanish** came, they made **AyAy** their fair game.
The **Dutch and English** arrived the same time,
And each decided, **"AyAy** is mine."
So, they grouped themselves and worked together,
And settled the islands like birds of a feather.

Later came the **French** like a hurricane,
And captured **St. Croix** and began to reign.
Religious men called Knights of Malta,
Got St. Croix as a gift from St. Christopher:
But poor management from the Knights,
Caused **St. Croix** to smother its lights.

So here comes **Denmark in 1733,**
And helped **St. Croix** to develop with glee.
Then forced the islands to labor for free.

Now the seventh flag that owns the isles,
Is the **red, white, and blue** that soars the skies.
Twenty-five million pieces of gold
He paid the **Danes** to relinquish their hold.
Which makes this island paradise,
A nice place to settle, to serve, and suffice.

Revised

The Caribbean Islands

The islands of the Caribbean
That's where the tourists go,
When they want to get away
From the freezing cold and snow.

They want to enjoy-
The sand, sea, and sun.
To experience the food,
The music, and lots of fun.

There are many islands in the group -
Yes, they are separated by water,
But all are united in the love -
Of their individual culture.

The islands come in many sizes,
Some are small and some are gigantic.
But together form the border of the Caribbean,
A sea that's an arm of the Atlantic.

There are several languages spoken here -
English, Spanish, French, and Dutch.
There are also local hybrid dialects,
Papiamento, Patois, Creole, and such.

So come and get to know our friendly people
We know you can't resist
Where should you visit first?
Well, you choose, I'll go down the list.

The majority of islands speak English
But most of these are small.
The biggest English speaker is Jamaica
Don't worry, I'll name them all.

There's Trinidad, Tobago, and Barbados
St. Kitts, Nevis, and Anguilla
Virgin Gorda, Jost Van Dyke
Anegada, Beef Island and Tortola.

St. Croix, St. John, and St. Thomas
The Cayman Islands, Antigua and Barbuda
St. Vincent and the Grenadines, Montserrat
St. Lucia, Dominica, and Grenada.

The Spanish islands are few
But they are huge… there's Cuba,
Puerto Rico and the Dominican Republic
A country on the island of Hispaniola.

On the western end of Hispaniola
The country of Haiti is in the French group
The other French islands include St. Martin
Martinique, St. Bartholomew, and Guadeloupe.

St. Martin's other side is called St. Maarten
Whose citizens are technically Dutch
But the people there speak English
You won't hear Dutch spoken much.

The two smallest Dutch gems
Are Saba and St. Eustatius
They speak English like their big brother
So, you don't have to put up a fuss.

The other Dutch ones are the ABC islands
Of Aruba, Bonaire, and Curacao
But even though they know Dutch
They speak a language they call Papiamento.

So come for a relaxing visit
Here you can enjoy God's creation
Return to your home refreshed and
Come next year for another Caribbean vacation.

By: Colin Curtis Hanley

Americans With Caribbean Roots: Famous Black Americans With Caribbean Connections.

Malcolm X, Grenada, human rights activist, and minister.

Louis Farrakhan, St. Kitts, religious leader who never quits.

Harry Belafonte, Jamaica, King of Calypso award and singer.

Sydney Poitier, Bahamas, first Black actor to win Academy Awards. He's one of my favorite black heroes.

Colin Powel, Jamaica, civilian who found his roots in Africa.

Cecily Tyson, Nevis, Award-winning actress, starred in the Roots series. Relative of Sister Sheila Wilson.

Tim Duncan, Anguilla, champion basketball coach and player.

Billy Dee Williams, Montserrat, American actor and aristocrat.

Jon Lucien, Virgin Isle, vocalist, sang "Shadow of a Smile."

Terrence Todman, St. Thomas, Career Ambassador to six (6) countries and American Diplomat.

Eric Williams, Trinidad and Tobago, historian, first Prime Minister in his country.

And our own Winston James Wilson, Army Veteran, and Virgin Islands Police Director.

OTHER US BLACKS AND THEIR CAREERS.

Thurgood Marshal, lawyer and former Associate Justice of the Supreme Court and later became its First Black Judge.

Condolezza Rice, American diplomat, political scientist, civil servant, and professor. First woman Security Advisor to the President and Secretary of State.

Colin Powel, civilian and soldier, statesman, diplomat who earned seven Presidential Awards and Medals for outstanding work. Secretary of State serving two presidents.

Martin Luther King, Baptist minister, Civil rights Leader, Drum Major for Justice, and died for the Cause.

Rosa Parks' refusal to give up her seat on the bus started the Civil Rights Movement. Honored as first lady of civil rights and mother of the freedom movement.

Elijah Cummings, law maker, politician, civil rights advocate, and patriotic humanitarian.

John Lewis, American politician and statesman, Civil Rights Activist, saw segregation and isolation.

Barack Hussein Obama, politician, author, retired attorney, elected first Black President of the United States of America. Served two terms.

A Tribute
To The President:

B – Best man God has placed, to
A – Answer the call, for a
R – Race he has to run, and be
A – Able to achieve another chance to change, and the
C – Courage to face the challenge, for
K – Knowledge and kindness are the keys.

H – Humble   **O**- Organized
U – Unique   **B** – Bold
S – Successful   **A** - Active
S- -Super   **M** - Memorable
E – Educated   **A** – Ambassador
I - Intelligent
N- New Blood

There is no authority except from God, and the authorities that exist are appointed by God.

Romans 13:1

The Last Days

MR. Barack Obama, president number
forty-four
Has now walked through the open door
A daunting task he has to face,
For God has put him in that place.
To rescue and restore the economy
With billions of stimulus money
That will aid us on the road to recovery.

Banks need the bailout to keep the money flowing
Allowing businesses to keep the jobs a-coming,
And consumers encouraged to continue their spending.
These are all factors that fuel the synopsis
Of the Global Economic Crisis.

Though taxes may decrease and wars increase
Though the auto industry threatens bankruptcy,
And newspapers claim insolvency.
Though homeowners fear foreclosures,

Though the Stock Market plunges and plummets,
Though swindlers fake and "Made-off"
And with our life savings take off.
Thus, forming a vicious cycle in this recession-
Causing families to plunge into deeper depression.

Surely there must be a workable solution
That will bring about a healthy infusion.
For housing, health, and education
Are paramount in making a wealthy nation.

NOW, according to God's word and creed
Perilous times are here indeed
For living in these last days, we read
That men are vile and full of greed.
Making merchandise of us with themes
Of lying talks and made-up schemes.
And not just without, but even within
For all have come short and are prone to sin.

But no longer does their judgment linger,
For destruction is at the tip of their finger.
Yes, the Lord, He knows their number,
And neither does He sleep or slumber.
So, let us be vigilant, be sober and take a stand,
For, **THE DAY OF THE LORD** is close at hand.

(Based on 2 Timothy 3:1-5; 2 Peter 2:1-3; 2 Thessalonians 2:1-3)

Christmas

Christmas Joys

The Advent of Christmas shows us **Love**
What a wonderful blessing from above
God so loved us that He gave his Son
As a precious gift to everyone.

Christmas also speaks of **Joy**
Shepherds were told of the Baby Boy
Lying on a bed there in that manger
Was that glorious little stranger.

Instead of war we need the **Peace**
Our Savior came to bring
And goodwill that will never cease
As we laugh and pray and sing.

Another attribute is the **Hope** he gives
That He will come again
To take His children home to live
Forever and to reign.

Love, Joy, Peace and Hope
Are wonderful gifts of God!
So, cherish the blessing, never mope
As we worship Christ our Lord.

JESUS IS ALL WE NEED!

Christmas on the secular side
Spins with a different tide
Replaces love with lust
Thinking merchandise is a must.

Being happy replaces joy
Not only because of the Christmas toy
The music and the dancing masquerade
And crowds following like a parade.

The world's peace is hard to reach
War and anguish are what they teach
Their peace is just an outward show
For on the inside life is ready to blow.

Their hope is for the best
But their life is just a mess
It is coiled up like a rope
There's no way they can really cope.

Love, joy, peace, and hope
Can bring them much despair
As we watch on television, the soaps
We can see they definitely do not care.

PUT CHRIST BACK IN CHRISTMAS

Creative Writings

Creative Writings:

JESUS CHRIST the Almighty Lord,
Our Messiah and Son of God
Has come to earth salvation to bring.
Let us rejoice and joyfully sing
Hallelujah to our King!

A host of angels proclaimed His birth
Telling men, the Messiah has come to earth,
To free us from our bondage of sins
And His salvation to us brings.

He gives wisdom, mercy, and love
Everything good is promised from above
Eternal life, lasting peace, and worship always
Inspire only our thanks and praise.

Holy Ghost our teacher be,
Guardian Spirit and helper He.
Powerful gift from heaven sends
For all who believe - brothers, sisters, and friends.

12/26/08

Song: We Wise Saints

We wise saints of Bovoni are
Bearing gifts from near and far
O'er hills and hi-ways, valleys, and bi-ways
Following Christ our Star.

CHORUS:
Oh, God of wonder, God of might
God our heavenly star shines bright
Still guiding shepherds, and heralding sinners
To that wondrous Christmas Light.

Praise we bring to honor our King
Prayer we ask to accomplish the task.
Blessing and honor, wisdom, and power,
Our worship to Christ we sing.

Thanks to God our heavenly Lord
For all good gifts that we enjoy.
Work and wealth, and food and health
His favors we all employ.

Jesus Christ our living word
Is the best we have ever heard!
Preaching, teaching, healing, leading
Witnessing, studying - we must be heeding.

06/06/08

(Tune: We Three Kings)

God Has Spoken ...
Hebrews 1:1-3

God spoke to Jewish Christians in times past
By visions, dreams, and signs it was vast
But in these last days he speaks through His Son
Jesus Christ, the blessed and holy One.

Gentiles are adopted in the great scheme of things
This is what the mystery of the Church brings
The virgin birth, the suffering Christ, salvation for all mankind
Is exactly what the Creator had in mind!

Prophets of old could not understand
The message they brought to fallen man.
Angels also longed to experience the thrills
The joy of salvation which the Holy Spirit instills.

Jesus taught from the Mount in Galilee
The Beatitudes which are what our attitude should be
Thankfulness, forgiveness, humility and compassion
While spreading the Good News: That is our mission.

God gave His Son as a special gift
From sin our friends, enemies, and neighbors to lift
Love, joy, hope, mercy, and peace
Are attributes that will never cease!

SONG: O God our help in ages past
    Our hope for years to come
    Be Thou our guide while life shall last
    And our eternal home.

... SO, LET THE CHURCH SAY AMEN!

The Beauty
Of A Milestone

That is the time we reflect on the past
To see how far we have come at last
Our future we must surely embrace
While with patience we run this race.

Fifty years of service, of fellowship and praise
Fifty years of witness, our loyalty we raise.
Fifty years to sing and to bring -
Honor and worship to our King.

It is the time of Jubilee, to show who we can truly be
A time to love and to forgive, a time to really and truly live.
A time to heal, a time to share a meal.
No time for ranks, but a time to give thanks.

For all the gifts that we enjoy,
For all the memories we employ
For the talents God to us has given
And for the blessed hope of heaven.

Get rid of the boredom, enjoy the freedom
Our fathers fought to gain - despite all anguish, toil, and pain.
No more embarrassing feeling, this is the time for healing
The past is gone, the future has come.

So let go of the anger and the fighting
Let go of the languor and the backbiting
Let go of the pride and the jealousy
For this is **the year of Jubilee!**

**Written to celebrate the 50th Anniversary of
Bovoni Baptist Church 12-14-14**

Bovoni Baptist Church

Forty-three years ago, I left my homeland
Came to St. Thomas at my mother's command
Lived in Bovoni, my two sons and I
And worshipped together in the church nearby.

We learned many important truths
Which were already taught to us as youths
Attended Sunday-School and the services too,
And our commitment to God we did renew.

After High School my children left here
To college they went to pursue their career
But on returning they changed their course
Travelled elsewhere and that without force.

Baptized and committed I stayed on
In various ministries, I served the Son
Witnessing, teaching, singing and cleaning,
Testifying and thanking God for my healing.

Missionaries came from far and near
With the Good News of salvation to bear.
Many turned from the darkness of night
To Jesus Christ, the one true Light.

Christians must be on the move to revive
And keep the Church of Jesus Christ alive.
While humbly making believers of every nation
So, peace and love may reign on every occasion.

Believers should have the mindset of Christ
Showing compassion, selflessness and love,
Telling how Jesus has paid the ultimate price
To redeem for us a new life with Him above.

Miscellaneous

My Challenge:

May 19, 2013, I had my yearly mammogram
The year before nothing was seen on the diagram
But after taking the picture a second time
I knew it wasn't going to be just fine.

A biopsy confirmed the suspicion
So, I had to make a quick decision
"No chemo," said my mother, before she died.
But a tongue lashing from Dr. Rosenberg, I almost cried.

Two lumps I was told, and they are small
I won't have to do any chemo at all
A lumpectomy would be the surgery
And would require only radiation therapy.

But when the results of the surgery came
It certainly had taken on another name.
HER2/neu is a protein that was positive
And ER/PR was one positive, one negative.

Chemo then was the preferred solution
So, I had to make a resolution
A second opinion was sought by fame
But the findings remained exactly the same.

Another surgery was scheduled to install
A medi--port inside the chest wall
To administer meds, fluids, and labs in a state
Which makes the procedure easier to tolerate.

I encountered minor discomforts for sure
Lack of appetite, tastelessness, and much more
Headache, heartburn, and also diarrhea,
Numb and tingling fingers, rashes, and loss of hair.

Friends and relatives prayed to God for me
They all helped in any and every capacity
Driving, feeding, caring, and sharing
I give God thanks for His loving and healing.

Doctors Comissiong, Bachan and Hughes are specialists
A surgeon, a chemotherapist and radiation oncologists.
Trained nurses and technicians enjoy their profession
And perform their duties with love and compassion.
Arnelle and Kimra used special skill
To manipulate the port without causing ill will.

So, I would encourage women everywhere
To treat their health with loving care
Many life issues will arise with age
And men also will fit this permanent stage.
So, exercise, immunize, eat healthy rations and no more
For God's love, favor and blessings are abundantly in store.

A poem inspired by the painting "The Tempest" by Janie Reed
Written by Jamilah Hanley, winner of the Humanities Festival Contest.

The Tempest

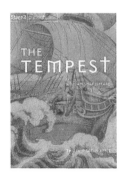

Oh, tempestuous ocean!
Which aptly disagrees with life and harmony.
Above looms a formidable sky
Filled to the brim with tears.
At once, a lightning bolt strikes with all
The despondency and rage of human years.

Deep below the ocean can be found in an uncanny calm,
While on shores of sand are violently dancing palms.
Your present state is a model mocking too
Our own demeanor and the way it can be derived.
The opposite is also true,
When we are hope and love deprived.

Oh, tempestuous ocean!
What can be attributed to your current state?
Is it born of arduous desire, or malevolent hate?
Can this be from all the injustices?
You have witnessed throughout the years?
Or is it Poseidon's way of periodically invoking all our fears?

There are untold stories on the outer banks of the seas,
Some of which are filled with lustful and decadent fantasies.
Most that deals with the avarice and folly of mankind;
The type that makes purity and virtue an impossibility to find.

Oh, tempestuous sea!
Is there any hope of justice in sight?
Are we doomed to live constantly in greed and villainy?
Rage on relentless: Prompt us to do what's right.

Jamilah Hanley

That Fateful Friday Night: April 17, 2015

This is murder my brother!

My friend should not have been brutally killed
On reaching his home which he recently build.
Friday nights were his social time with us boys
Meeting friends, neighbors and coworkers were sure joys.

But others had something very different in view.
Was it jealousy, hatred or political strumu and todo?
Could it be that he was getting too close
To uncover the money-laundering criminals – a host?

Who gives you the authority to take another's life?
And making it seem like a robbery and meaningless strife?
Top-notch officials also seem to be involved
Is that why up to now it has gone unsolved?

And it makes our all-wise, all-knowing God very sad.
For His eyes roam to and fro, beholding the good and the bad.
So, confess and repent for judgment is now at hand.
If not, you WILL wander the streets like a miserable vagabond.

Rest in peace, Everette, my friend –
Our Lord, He knows how they will end.
A Grieving Friend

TO ALL OF US:
Remember: Life is short, but death is sure
We must be certain to keep our hearts pure.
For when it is time to meet our Maker
Be sure God will know if we are a faker.

Be An Overcomer!

God's Miracle:

It was a Wednesday evening in November
When we arrived at church for Bible study and prayer
And even before we sat in the pews
We heard the devastating news.
He was only doing an honest day's work
With his students as their football coach.
Our dear Brother Sherman was knocked down by car.
And was rushed by ambulance to the Intensive Care.
He was in a coma suffering from life-threatening injuries
Which required immediate surgeries.
Attached to numerous gadgets needed to supply
Medication and sustenance for healing to apply.
Some went to the hospital to abide at his side
Others stayed at church and prayed that night.
Trusting God to make everything alright.
Friends and relatives took turns to stay
With him throughout the night and day.
Looking for any sign and motion
That would reveal his state and condition.
After some time, his eyes he opened,
Squeezed a hand or a word he muttered.
We rejoiced with hallelujah thanks and praise
For the blessed hope of living now raise.
He later confessed he had no knowledge or idea
That he even had Schneider Regional hospital care.
But at Jackson Memorial where he was transferred
More movements were visible, and memory stirred.

Brother Sherman is a living testimony of faith and prayer,
And God's love, grace and hope we all can share.
With a celebration at Christmas with friends and family
Doctors were sure he will have a great recovery.
THANK YOU LORD!

12 /12/14

He Is Special

Brother Sherman was born to special parents
Who raised him with love and Christian forbearance
He trusted Christ at an early age
And at three years was ready to preach on stage.

Brother Sherman is a special young man
Who strives to do the best that he can
To coach the young players in his charge
So, they will do well winning big and large.

Brother Sherman had a special dream
To play on his college football team
He tried and trained and passed the test
But many setbacks delayed the rest.

Brother Sherman is a special person
A youth leader and a Christian for certain
A man of prayer which gave him power
To help in that crucial hour.

We give God thanks for Brother Sherman
Who grew up to be a special gentleman
We pray for continued attitudes and attributes
And principles the 'Fruit of the Spirit' institutes.

Friends and relatives are here to enjoy
All God's blessings His servants employ
And as we celebrate this special occasion
We worship you Lord for Your bountiful provision.

A day of remembrance, a day of praise
A day to give thanks, our voices we raise
So, let us rejoice and be glad in it
For the Lord our God he made these days.
WE LOVE YOU BROTHER SHERMAN!

No testing has overtaken you that is not common to man. God is faithful, and he will not suffer you to be tempted above that you are able; but with the temptation also make a way of escape, that you may be able to bear it. 1 Corinthians 10:13

Be An Overcomer!

The year 2014 was a miraculous one
For through many dangers God sent his Son
To protect His children from the evil one.
And glorious victories have been won. **HALLELUJAH!**

Satan comes to steal our joy
And our family he tries to destroy.
But our faith he cannot kill
If we refuse to yield to his will. AMEN!

First, she fell and broke her leg
In two places, no less, it was a big mess.
It took three months of pain and surgeries
Satan you cannot win, she is free of injuries.

Next came the accident with the car
While going to worship the one true Star
Satan, you lose, no-one was hurt
So go back and slither in the dirt.

Then came November and all hell broke loose
His eyes set on two he must capture in his noose.
The one in a coma, he's sure he will win,
The other overturned and hanging by a string.

But God is in the midst of everything
No disaster, no calamity, or any other thing
Can defeat His perfect saving plan
Or the healing He brings to fallen man.

THANK YOU LORD!

Other aches and pains through the years are all evidence
That Satan is at work with much persistence
Aching backs, knees, legs: fish poisoning and blood clots
But we refuse to adhere to Satan's devious plots.
We SHALL overcome by prayer and fasting too
And with endurance we must and shall pursue!

For God is in the midst of everything
No tragedy, no catastrophe, or any other thing
Can defeat His perfect will and plan
Or the healing He brings to fallen man.
Thank you Lord!

So, as we stand on the portal of the opening year
May we greet it with love, joy, and good cheer.
Let us continue onward as children of the day
Knowing that God's Word will never pass away.

Tributes

Poetic Memoirs
Part 2

To The Newly-Elected President Trump:

There is no authority except from God: and the
authorities that exist are from God. Romans 13:1

"GOD'S SOVEREIGN WILL"

"Make America Great Again!"
Was the theme for Mr. Trump's campaign.
Yes, he is president number forty-five
And he has promised to keep hope alive.
For ISIS would be gone at last,
And terrorism, a thing of the past.

No more Muslims whose creed we cannot understand
No more Mexicans who once owned the land.
No more rapists, murderers, or drug addicts.
No more criminals, no more private E-mail intervals.
No more rigged election, causing suspicion and contention.
No need to suspect Russia's interference or hacking,
For Wiki Leaks will confess and send all suspicions packing.
And no more fake news nor vicious and harmful views.

We will build the wall both strong and tall
And the price they pay will be My call.
Refugees will be forcefully and carefully screened
Telling where they have been and what they have seen.

The economy will definitely recover,
For jobs he can and will deliver.
Businesses will return from foreign lands,

And non-taxpayers receive severe reprimands.
We will all respect and obey the laws
And not hide under some bankruptcy clause.
For Presidents and aspirants all make known
And voluntarily reveal their tax return.
President Trump will be our leader
We must show respect though not a believer.
The daunting task he will not face
For fellow Republicans will be in place,
To keep him focus on the plan
His predecessor could not demand.
Health, insurance, college fees, and immigration
Are real issues that are facing the nation,
And can be solved with proper education.

Some view this poem as being in agreement
But it is just reviewing his comments and statement
And merely being sarcastic since he is so bombastic.
For preaching racism, violence, and hate
Followers are bound to imitate and emulate.
Ignorance, Prejudice and Racism! What attitude
To preside over the nation's magnitude!
The slogan "Make America Great Again"
Really means "Make America WHITE Again."
Nevertheless, let us pray for guidance, wisdom, and strength
That empathy be shown throughout the length.
God has a way of forwarding His plan,
Even by divisive means of man, He can.
So, let us be vigilant, be sober, pray and stand still,
And see how God fulfills His Sovereign Will.

God is in His holy temple, let all the earth keep silent before Him.
Habakkuk 2:20

God is working His purpose out, as year succeeds to year.
God is working His purpose out, and the time is drawing near.
Nearer and nearer draws the time: The time that shall surely be.
When the earth shall be filled with the Glory of God As the waters
cover the sea.

Hymn by: Arthur Campbell Ainger, 1841-1919
10/31/2017

To the Memory of our dear Sister Sonia A. Aubrey
on this first anniversary of her passing on October 17, 2017

Precious Memories:

A year has come and gone, but her memory lingers on!
Sister Aubrey was a faithful and devoted member
The Ladies Vice-President, and angelic singer
When I left to attend my grandchildren's graduation
She organized the Father's Day lunch celebration.

A Board member, Awana Instructor and Florist
Arranged Carnations for Mother's Day from her business
Vocalist in the Choir coupled with the Worship Team
That melodious voice that made us beam.
As she ministered during the Lord's Supper,
We are assured she belongs in heaven's choir.

A champion for the MENTALLY ILL cause,
President and Founding Member of the NAMI clause
To duties and responsibilities she always tend
And ministered at Shulterbrandt until the end.
But even though illness took her away
We give God thanks for a successful stay.

She was a Praying Woman!
She was a Faithful Christian!
She was a Loving and caring Wife!
 A Devoted Mentor and Friend!
A Pioneer for Mental Health Care!
And a truly Phenomenal Woman!
May she rest in Eternal Peace!

10/17/2018

Hurricanes

Two Angry Women
Irma And Maria

The hurricanes came hurriedly by
Did their damage and left us high and dry
Meaning we were flooded and stranded.
The one from the East: the other from the West
So strong was their force, we had no recourse
But to stand the test, and hope for the best.

The devastation was enormous
To count the cost is simply ridiculous
Three schools must be demolished
Causing regular sessions to be abolished.
For double sessions, a thing of the past
Has come back to haunt schools at last.
Irma and Maria should be fined and confined
And then cut their presumptuous behind.
Imagine coming with two Category Five
Their plan was that we should not survive
And even though they rant and rave
God was in the midst to help and save.
Their counterparts decide to visit each year
And though unwelcome, we still prepare.
But such magnitude was unheard of before
So, the building code will have to improve some more.

As it has been said again and again
We are resilient and will not complain.
Let us be kind and help each other
And have respect one for another.
We won't worry about a thing
Just pray, and praise God and sing.
Thanking Him for the rising sun
And every day from now on.
 TO GOD BE THE GLORY!

9/17/2017

Facing Two Hurricanes Was A Chilling Experience For My Granddaughter!

This traumatic experience was truly frightening
Causing her to consider abandoning her schooling.
The crying in bed all day, and the urge to run away
Took encouragement and counselling to get her to stay.

Just two more subjects for graduation
She then completed her High School education
Finally got her chance to leave the island
And on to Harvard she now takes her stand.

A happy camper is she at last
Training and studying to do well in class
Trusting Jehovah she cannot fail
Striving to emulate Florence Nightingale.

5/30/2018

The Dancing Trees

It was fun to watch the fruitful trees
Dancing and prancing in the brisk breeze
The excitement was inviting and tantalizing
And gale force winds, so very frightening
But I stayed and enjoyed the scene some more
Until stronger winds forced me indoor.

The howling winds and the pounding rains
Were sure to cause tremendous pains.
The sounds resonated throughout the night
As we huddled together in sudden fright.

The blue water tank emerged with glee
And had a little jig with the peas tree
Then disappeared happily over the wall
As if heeding an exuberant call.
The destruction we saw when morning light came
It's hard to believe they're now springing again.
Remember the miracle of Aaron's rod
For sure we know there is a God. GIVE HIM PRAISE!

2017

Two years later, here comes Dorian
Being disobedient - did not follow the plan
Changing course here, there, and everywhere
Determined we should not have a good year.
Rushed on us with a Category 1
But even minor damage is no fun.
The Bahama Islands got it really bad
To see the devastation is so very sad.
So, we are determined to do our part.
To help the residents get a new start.
    MAY God protect us all!

Covid - 19

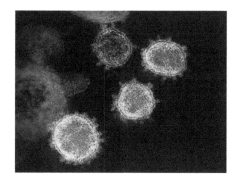

The Virus:

COVID 19! What is it? Nobody knows!
A virus that dished out deadly blows?
In 2019 corona decided to start
With no idea when it will depart.
To the world this pandemic came
And many lives it did claim. But who's to blame?

Persons with compromise immune system
Are all unexpectedly falling victim.
Asthma, diabetes, shortness of breath
Have resulted in multiple uncontrollable deaths.

Have a heart! Our lungs are at risk
Dry cough, sore throat, blood clots - a list
That plays out on this disastrous disc.
Coping with all this fear and anxiety
Only God can give us the victory.
I have it, you have it, it is hard to tell
So take precaution, so we'll all be well.
Wash hands often, don't touch your face
Wear a mask, and stand six feet apart.
    Be wise, sanitize.

Testing needs to be administered left and right
Trying to win the war in this terrible fight.
Ventilators too are desperately in need
For normal breathing process to succeed.
    Do your exercise and energize!

Expert officials have no idea when
A vaccine will be made to help all men.
So, let's pray for wisdom from God above
Who always showers us with His love.

First responders selflessly intercede
To aid suffering seniors combat the disease.
Nursing homes first showed signs of deadly attacks
With lives succumbing to warlike contacts.
Headaches, fever, muscle aches and pains too,
Are part of a novel corona that's new
But chayote, garlic, lemon, ginger, onion and more
Aloe, lemongrass, coconut and olive oil for sure,
Are natural remedies abundantly in store.
Could be the beginning of a wonderful miracle cure!

With businesses closed and everyone on lockdown
Many are longing to explore the town.
Going to the beach and having much fun
While soaking up Vitamin D in the summer sun.

We pray for those who labor on the frontline
Showing brotherly love with hearts that bind.
Let us also show love, and care for each other
Brother, sister, father, and mother.

The peace of God all understanding passes
Is offered to all mankind, classes and masses;
So, confess, repent and ask God's forgiveness
Humble ourselves, come before Him with meekness.
     BE A BLESSING!

Virtual reality is the 'new normal'
Nothing anymore would be formal.
No stylish clothes and manly pose.
For housedresses and pajamas
Are now the real charmers.
So, stay at home, enjoy your work
And students, be diligent, do not shirk.

May 2020

What A Life:
What A World:
What A Time!

The above title was coined many years ago
And this relevant chorus we still do echo.

Father, we thank you for your great creation
You've helped to develop this wonderful nation.
Help us to use wisdom in what we do and say
That we may grow in knowledge day by day.

President Trump was justly impeached
But acquittal from office could not be reached.
Republicans vowed he could do no wrong
So, they banned together and made him strong.
Abuse of Power was clearly a crime
And *quid pro quo* was revealed in due time.
One Senator, upholding his conviction, took a stand,
But Obstruction of Congress he could not demand.
The Public Trust has been compromised,
And spiritually speaking, we've been victimized.

12/18/2019

And The Saga Goes On!
Corona Has Come!

Have you heard of the "invisible enemy"
A virus that changed our destiny?
"For people are dying *in galore*
Who have never *even* died before!"

Let the dead past bury its dead
In the Bible it has been said.
But no public viewing, no mass gathering
Has become a sad and scary situation.

Hydroxychloroquine, disinfectant, and ultra-violet light
Could be ingested to combat this deadly fight.
'Try it, try it! What you have to lose?'
Stop making senseless, and idiotic excuse.

Have you heard of social distancing?
No hugging, no kissing nor handshaking,
Put on your mask and stand six feet apart
You can laugh but cover your cough.
Please have a heart and do your part!

Medical staff are doing their utmost
Care takers too are always at their post
Sacrificing their lives while attending sick patients
And quarantine families thanking God for deliverance.
    Thank you Lord!

"For I know the plans I have for you," declares the Lord, "plans to
prosper you and not to harm you,
plans to give you hope and a future." Jeremiah 29: 11 NIV

4/15/2020

The Puppet

How pathetic is it that VP *Trense*
Acts as if he has no common sense.
Or maybe he just lacks intelligence.
Came to the office as a believing Christian
But proves merely to be a practicing politician.
Monkey see, monkey do! Imagine,
The bottle of water removed from the table
Mimicked – he must be unstable!
CDC guidelines pamphlet held up high
Attributed to Trump at briefing, is a big lie.
Health precautions are what he teaches
Yet unwilling to practice what he preaches.
Is wearing a mask, a copying task?
Even though they claim to be evangelicals
Just proves, some *POP's* lack true morals.

4/28/2020

The Sin Of The Skin:

There's a knee in my neck, I cannot breathe
'Twas George Floyd's desperate and dying plead
But officers looking on, gave no heed.
So, in agony he died - as was seen worldwide.

Angry mobs took to the streets
Rioting, burning and looting businesses
Protesting injustice, racism, and murder
This can't be allowed to escalate further!

Despite four officers' heartless activity
Others knelt in respect and solidarity
To show regret for this devastating scene
A sign of humility, and repentance it has been.

Thank You Lord for creating us in Your image
Loving, kind, forgiving, and free of scrimmage.
Spreading the Good News of a joyful life within
So, we won't be guilty of 'the sin of the skin'.

6/4/2020

Skit: The Murder!

Characters: George, Cop, Mama
Setting: The Streets of Minnesota

George:	I can't breathe! I can't breathe!
Cop:	*Shut up!*
George:	Mama, help!
Mama:	What's happening, George?
George:	There's a knee in my neck.
Mama:	Well, push it off.
George:	I can't.
Mama:	Why not?
George:	I'm handcuffed.
Mama:	Where are you?
George:	On the ground.
Cop:	*You'll be here for a long time.*
Mama:	A long time! How long?
Cop:	*Eight minutes, forty-six seconds maybe more.*
Mama:	What! I'm calling the police.
Cop:	*(Laugh)* Ha! Ha! a!Ha!*I'm the police.*
George:	See you, Mama.
Song:	I am coming home, coming now to Thee,

Wash me, cleanse me in the blood that flowed from Calvary.

All Life Matters!

And the saga continues on and on and on...
When will we ever learn, when will we ever learn?

Does our white counterpart have no heart?
Don't they realize, they're killing us like flies?

Meet in the street, shot in the back
Even in our homes, the bullet comes.
How can we survive these deadly attacks?
When considered as nothing for we are just Blacks.

Black lives matter, of course! Without force,
Have they no remorse?
But all life matters right from the Source.

Where have all the brothers gone?
Gone to graveyards everyone.
When will they ever learn, when will they ever learn?

6/6/2020   What's next, only God knows

A Tumultious Year

2020 has been a tumultuous year
A novel virus we've all come to fear
It has no manners, it has no respect
No physical greeting, just plain neglect
But God is in the midst to love and protect.

Millions have died, the President lied
Let us do our part, take the warning to heart.
Wash your hands, stay six feet apart,
Wear your mask, cover your mouth and nose
Not just on the chin as a manner of repose.

Thanks to the scientists who with God's help
Have developed a vaccine to make us well
Though many try to refute its dependability
We trust God for its suitability.
2020, a year of vision
Taught us to make wise decisions
Do your research, read, read, read
Study the Word and do take heed.
Thank You, Lord!

A Dark Chapter in our Nation's History

Have you ever heard, have you ever seen,
How the President tried to redeem
An election which he clearly lost,
By instilling violence at any cost?

What should have been peaceful protesting,
Turned into mob rioting and hateful molesting.
Breaching the Capitol and forcing doors in
Breaking windows and scaling walls to get within.
Supporters were incited to become domestic terrorists.
Enabled with lies from a boss who's an insurrectionist,
Causing employers to hide and run for cover.
It has been a sad, sad day for America.

January 6th. The Day of Infamy!

Not Fit:

Donald trump, not fit to be called President,
Has embarrassed his party and the US residents.
Made a fool of his supporters and right-wing reporters.
Shame on you for swallowing his lies,
Instead of embracing honest goodbyes.
Imagine two busloads of evangelicals,
Who journeyed to Washington and became radicals?
What were you thinking, have you no sense?
You even meant to murder loyal Mike Pence.

What do you expect your reward will be?
When you stand before God in eternity.
To account for what was taught in your ministry.
Trump can't save you, it would be too late,
If you both experience the same exact fate
And end up in that awfully horrible place.
Be wise, don't compromise, run the race with grace.
What should have taken place long before,
Has now been realized by many more.
The only president impeached twice,
With a trial in place, a conviction would be nice.

But it was not to be, most republicans are scared,
Of the monster they created they now feared.
So, they ignored the truth and thought it just fine,
To buckle to pressure, for their career's on the line.
Imagine getting punished for telling the truth.
And sanctioning those who stood firmly to boot.
By refusing to prove the origin of the lies
But refute the truth and try to get by.
Trump republic is a terrible example,
That no one should continue to sample.

A Dream Come True!

History has been made in 2021,
An Asian Indian and a Black American
A career woman with Caribbean roots
Whose determination produced many fruits.
Attorney General of California, and advocate
And United States Presidential candidate.
A lawyer, a senator, and district attorney
Now Vice President almost completes the journey.
Despite all odds she kept climbing the ladder
Where intriguing girls would all like to aspire.
Who is this notable woman of fame?
Kamala Harris is her name.

A Tribute: Two Historic Firsts

Forty-sixth President, Joseph R. Biden,
is a career politician,
With thirty-six years of service and genuine devotion.
As a senator who at thirty was then the youngest,
And a President who at seventy-eight is now the oldest.
Truly a great treasure that none can measure.
Not forgetting eight years as vice President
And many other duties involving that resident.
Now as President many challenges lie ahead,
But with determination he faces them without dread
Trusting God for wisdom and guidance instead.
Pandemic, failing economy, suffering citizens and more,
Enemies on every hand, as he tries to heal the land.
But focusing on God he will always stand sure,
May God bless his leadership with peace galore.
    God Bless America!

Our Presidents

First the Lofty Washington,

That noble, great, and a mortal one.
The elder **Adams next** we see,
And **Jefferson** comes number **three.**
Then **Madison is fourth** you know,
The **fifth** one on the list, **Monroe:**
The **sixth, then Adams** comes again,
And **Jackson, seventh**, in the train.
Van Buren, eighth upon the line,
And **Harrison** counts **number nine.**
The **tenth is Tyler** in his turn,
And **Polk the eleventh** as we learn;
The **twelfth is Taylor** in rotation,
The **thirteenth, Fillmore** in succession;
The **fourteenth, Pierce** has been selected,
Buchannan, fifteenth is elected.
Sixteenth, Lincoln rules the nation,
Johnson A. seventeenth, fills the station.
As the **eighteenth, Grant,** two terms serves,
Nineteenth, Haynes our honor preserves.
Twentieth, Garfield becomes our head,
Twenty-first, Arthur succeeds the dead.
Then **Cleveland** next was selected,
Twenty-third, Harrison is elected.
Twenty-fourth, Cleveland is recalled.
Twenty-fifth, McKinley twice installed,
Twenty-sixth, T. Roosevelt, strenuous, firm.
Taft, twenty-seventh, serves his term.
Twenty-eight, Wilson holds the place,
A nation's problems he has to face.

Selected

Other Presidents:

Twenty-ninth, Harding had two firsts,
Calvin, thirtieth, won women's right to vote.
Thirty-first, Hover saw the Great Depression;
F. Roosevelt, thirty-second,
in a four-term succession,
Led nation to World War 2 revolution.
Thirty-third, Truman used Atomic Bomb tactics,
Causing Japan to surrender its antics.
Thirty-fourth came **Eisenhover** to integrate schools,
Thirty-fifth, JFK initiated Peace Corps and enforced the rules.
L. Johnson, thirty-sixth, provided health insurance to the elderly,
While **Nixon, thirty-seventh**, impeached – resigned scandalously.
Thirty-eighth, Ford, only president and vice-president not elected,
Pardoned Nixon and was rejected.
Thirty-ninth, Carter, winner of Nobel Peace Prize,
His term saw fifty-three US hostages heist.

Fortieth, Reagan's hostages for weapons exchanged,
East and West unite and the Berlin Wall deranged.
Bush Sr., forty-first, known for the Gulf War attack;
Clinton, forty-second, impeached – still managed to counteract;
National Debt reduced, the economy rescued and restored.

G. W. Bush, forty-third, presently serving second term contract,
Despite war in Iraq and homeland security attack.
No child left behind his plan to enhance the mind,
To improve and advance public schools,
And Social Security Reform improves.

Who would be next to stand the test?
The challenge he must face as he takes his place,
The right to impose and the wrong to oppose.
ONLY GOD KNOWS! (Composed 05/05/05)

And now we know. God grant him the
wisdom to accept Your wise council.

Forty-fourth, BARACK HUSSEIN OBAMA – God's chosen one
The people's choice for the native son,
A second term to cherish and four more years to relish.
Though a recession he inherits, yet his love exhibits merits.
Although opposed on every hand, true to God he'll firmly stand.

Donald J. Trump number fifty-five
Though twice impeached was still alive
Until the Electoral College had spoken
And the two-term prophecy was broken.

Fifty-sixth, Joseph R. Biden is such a dare,
Had no fear to make politics his chosen career.
Forty-four years in the bag and eight more to be had
Is a service-filled life that started as a lad.
GOD BLESS AMERICA!

Quiz: Can You Guess?

One term president, twice impeached, a cheat, a liar,
an insurrectionist and much more.
Intended message: Make America White Again.
WHO AM I? ....

Career politician, youngest senator at age 30, serving 36 years;
oldest president at age 78, and presently serving first term.
WHO AM I? ....

First African American president, one of the youngest, served
two-terms during which Asam Bin Ladin was assassinated.
WHO AM I? ....

First African- Asian -American Vice President.
Roots in India and the Caribbean; lawyer, senator,
attorney general, district attorney and more.
WHO AM I? ....

Youngest President served only two years before being
assassinated. Averted the Cuban Missile Crisis.
WHO AM I? ....

A Grandmother's Confession:

I have learned in whatsoever state I'm in therewith to be content.
Philippians 4:11

I AM JUST FINE

There is nothing wrong with me
I am as healthy as can be
I have arthritis in my knees and my back it aches
And when I talk, my voice trembles and shakes.
My fingers are numb, I cannot write,
But I'm perfectly well, won't give up the fight.
Arch support in my shoes for my feet
Else I won't be able to walk the street.
Sleep is sometimes denied at night
But each morning I find I am alright.
My memory is failing, my head's in a spin
But I'm awfully good for the state I'm in.
The moral is this as I unfold,
That for you and me we are growing old.
It's better to say "I'm fine with a grin
Than to tell them all the state we are in.
How do I know my youth is all spent?
Well, my get up and go just got up and went.
But I really don't mind when I think with a grin,
Of all the grand places my get up has been.

Old age is golden, I've heard it said,
But sometimes I wonder as I get into bed.
With my ears in a drawer, my teeth in a cup,
My eyes on the table, but still I wake up.
Before sleep dims my eyes, I say to myself,
"Is there anything I should put on the shelf
O yes, I remember to take out the hair
If not, what would this bald head wear?"

When I was young my slippers were red,
I could lift my heels up over my head.
When I grew up my moccasins were brown,
I could walk to school from country to town.
But now I'm old my sneakers are black
I walk down the hill, then huff and puff my way back.

I get up every morning and collect my wits
Then listen to the radio for funeral obits.
If my name is not read, then I know I'm not dead.
So, I get a good breakfast and go back to bed.

> *Thank You Lord!*

Revised and patterned after the original in Grandma's Girl.

I can do all things through Christ who strengthens me.

> **Philippians 4:13**

Prayer:

Merciful God and loving heavenly Father
In the name of Jesus Christ our elder Brother
We humble approach your throne of grace
And graciously bow before your face
Thanking You for forgiveness of sins
And all the blessings your salvation brings.
Divers ailments and diseases you're still healing
And the peace of mind that we're feeling
Thanks for the love of family and friend
And relationships if broken You can mend
Thanks also for your provision and protection
Supplying our needs and guarding our seeds.
 Loving the hopeless and caring for the homeless.
Protect our mind from permanent memory loss
And help us to always focus on You, our Boss.
    Forever and ever. Amen

I WAS BORN IN Charlestown, Nevis
Dedicated and served in the Charlestown Methodist Church
Attended the Charlestown Girls' Primary School
And the Charlestown Secondary School (CSS)
Graduated with a Cambridge School Certificate
Taught at Brown Hill Primary School
Mother of two boys and later grandmother of four girls
Pre-school teacher and after-school tutor
Migrated to St. Thomas, United States Virgin Islands
Rededicated my life to Christ and was baptized
Worship and serve in the Bovoni Baptist Church
Worked at Jane E. Tuitt Elementary School in the capacity of Teacher's Assistant.
Earned credits at the College of the Virgin Islands (CVI)
Retired from the Government of the Virgin Islands in 2004.

THE END